BASIC DOG TRAINING WITHOUT TREATS

by
DARREN

AuthorHouse™ UK Ltd.
500 Avebury Boulevard
Central Milton Keynes, MK9 2BE
www.authorhouse.co.uk
Phone: 08001974150

First published by AuthorHouse 11/21/2008

ISBN: 978-1-4389-0956-1 (sc)

Printed in the United States of America
Bloomington, Indiana

This book is printed on acid-free paper.

authorHOUSE®

Contents

INTRODUCTION

I have been training dogs for a long time now, and over the years I have often wondered why owners & trainers use treats to train a dog to do something you ask it to do. It's called bribery!!! So if I said to you sit and I will give you a £1 then of course you will sit a 100 times as you will get £100 it's the same with dogs.

I have devised training methods over the years without using treats and so now I pass on my knowledge to you hoping that you will understand my way is better.

A dog is a dog not a human so don't treat your dog like a human. Too many people I train treat their dogs like humans and wonder why they don't get results or wonder why their dog is a pack leader and not them.

In this book I will explain to you in easy step by step instructions what to do with illustrated pictures.

A good way to remember anything is by the letters C A P

Command
Action
Praise

Remember, a well trained dog is a happy dog.

SPECIAL THANKS TO

Helen Miles & Rachel Parsons
Charlie the Retriever & owner
Alfie Claire & family
Jack the Ridgeback & family
Bollinger the Labradoodle & family
Kyzo the Staffy
Cheryl Standing

CHOOSING THE RIGHT DOG

Choosing the right dog for you can be a daunting task, getting it wrong can lead to household disruptions in a big way. Do not choose a dog just because it has those loveable puppy eyes that look sad, or just because someone said these breeds are so easy to train because every dog is different.

1st take these things into consideration.

Why am I getting a dog?

Do I need a dog?

Am I working all day?

Can I walk the dog for at least 20 minutes twice a day?

Can I afford a dog?

Have you got any other pets?

Have you got children?

Do you live in a flat or house?

Do you have a garden?

Do you want an older dog or puppy?

Shall I have a rehomed dog or not?

Have I got the patience for a dog?

Can I afford to get the dog insured?

Can I afford the vet bills?

These are basic questions you need to ask yourself and if you are not sure *DO NOT GET ONE*.

But if you have thought about all the questions and still want one then here are a few tips on choosing a dog.

Whatever you decided to do, whether it's a rehomed dog or a private sale, remember, every breed is different in it's own way. I am a great believer in that the dog will choose it's owner, so let the dog decide.

Don't get a Collie if you live in a flat or can't walk as they need a lot of exercise, or a Staffy or Rottweiler because it makes you look tough. THINK!!!!!!!

Choose a dog to suit you and your personality. If you can't get around much then get a small dog that needs little exercise, but if you like to walk then go for an energetic dog, but remember all dogs need training whether they're 2 months old or 10 years old.

When you have chosen your dog, do not expect results straight away, remember there is a 2 month bonding period between humans and dogs – you get to know them and vice versa.

If you have decided on your dream dog, go to see it a few times before you take it away. If it's with parents, see the parents and ask for papers if any available. Do not let the owners say I will come to you as this means there is either something wrong with the dog or it is from a puppy farm. Always see the dog in it's own environment – that way you can see if it has any bad habits and what it is really like on it's own territory.

When taking a puppy away from it's parents, take a blanket with you and rub it over the mother and put the blanket in with the puppy so it feels safe and at least has its mothers smell and that way the dog will feel at least some comfort when you take it away.

If you have chosen a rehomed dog then go back and see it a few times before taking it away. If you have kids, take the kids to see it so you can see how it reacts with children and other members of the family. Take it for a walk, see how it handles and see if you can handle it as well. With rehomed dogs their background is always difficult to assess so you need as much information from the kennel owners as they can give you. Ask what they feed it on – you might want to change it but we will come to that later. See if it's chipped? Most dogs will be but make sure. Think about changing it's name as it might have bad memories with it's current name. Now you've chosen your dog you can get on with your training

Feeding Habits

The way you feed your dog can have an affect on your household and an affect on your dog. Feeding is very important in the household, it shows who is in charge.

What you feed your dog is very important too. I always suggest dry food for any dog and the best on the market is either Burns or James well Beloved. With no artificial colours or additives, it is pure natural food and if your dog is hyper then this will help calm them down. Remember if you're changing your dogs food, do it gradually over 2 or 3 days, don't just swap over food. Introduce the new food bit by bit as this will help to stop them getting upset stomach.

Feeding times are important. Never feed your dog 20 minutes before or after exercise as you could have problems. Have set times for feeding – If you feed your dog once a day then the best time is between 5pm and 7pm. If you feed twice a day then feed in morning between 7am and 9am and again at night but do not leave the food down all day. Your times may vary with your work but the important thing is to get into a routine.

Always when feeding, put your dogs dinner down and if they have not eaten within 20 minutes then take it away and throw it away as then they will have to wait until the next feeding time. Do not start to feel guilty if they have not touched their food as they will eat when they are hungry, and do not get into the habit of feeding treats if they are not eating. Leave them and they will eat.

You will find a balance on what your dog eats as they tend to eat more at night than in the morning, this is why feeding once a day is better.

Dogs need structure, and picking at their food is not good. You wouldn't let your family pick at bits all day, so don't let your dog.

When feeding, it is always a good idea to get your dog to leave and sit even for just a few seconds until you say eat, so that shows you are the alpha male.

Do not feed your dog at the table or let your dog eat human chocolate or food. I know they are your pet and look all cute and lovely, but they are dogs and should be treated as so.

HOUSE TRAINING

House training should be the first thing you teach your dog if not already done so. You don't need to go to the pet shop to buy nappies and bed mats as you have everything you need at home and it comes through the door free.

Firstly, get some newspaper and spread it around the kitchen area. Depending on the size of your kitchen, create an area of around 5ft square leading to the back door if you have one.

Everyday take some newspaper away so the area gets smaller, but if the dog has messed on the newspaper near the back door or anywhere else then replace that with new paper. When the area gets to around 2ft square start putting the newspaper outside the back door so the dog will realise he has to go outside.

When the dog does eventually go outside DO NOT give them treats but make sure you give them lots and lots of praise, and I mean lots of praise. Do not under any circumstances chastise your dog for messing in the house.

If your dog messes in the house, make sure you clean it up thoroughly and that the smell and odours are gone. If the ammonia is not cleaned up the dog will come to think it's their territory and will start marking it so.

Do not use bleach as it does not work!! - You need to use a strong antiseptic floor cleaner, like stain and odour remover.

Do not be afraid to praise your dog in public, as the dog will come to realise it's a good thing they are doing so will do it more often.

Always remember to carry doggy bags when you go out. A responsible owner will always clean up after their dog. If you see someone not cleaning up their mess, be a good owner and be polite and offer them a bag as they may not have any.

SITTING

Sitting is one of the easiest things you can get your dog to do. It's the first step in basic obedience and also the first step in household rules and respect from the dog.

To start with get your dog and just get him/her to stand by you (as in figure 1). By your left side is good as this is part of a structure which we will be doing later in C.A.P.

 FIGURE 1

FIGURE 2

With your left hand gently push down on the dogs rear and pull back on the lead so their head comes up. In a nice happy voice say SIT. Remember C.A.P (as in figure 2).

When the dog sits praise the dog a lot so they know it's a good thing for sitting. Don't give him/her a treat for doing so, as we want the dog to do it for you.

You need to do this three or four times in a row, but don't over do it as the dog will get bored and fed up. Only ask your dog to sit once – If they do not sit first time then do as shown in figures 1 and 2 again.

When out walking, make your dog sit at every kerb you come to and remember to give your dog praise when doing the sit.

Make your dog sit when giving them their food so they have to earn it.

Also before you take your dog out for a walk make them sit before you put the lead on so you are showing you are in control straight away.

Key Points
Place hand gently on dogs rear and push down gently
Pull head back at same time
Sit at every kerb
Sit before taking out for walk
Sit when feeding
Praise when doing a sit in a nice happy voice
C.A.P

DOWN

When a dog goes down it is a form of submission, which is why getting any dog to go down is hard and sometimes frustrating.

Ever wondered why when you tell them to go down they just stare at you as if to say, "ye rite pal, there's no way I'm going down, I'm the boss"? – Well that's a dogs way of saying "I'm in control not you". But here are a few things to help you get the dog to go down without treats.

One method is to put the lead on the dog and holding the lead close to the collar with the left hand pull down to the ground as shown in picture and say DOWN in a firm voice. Stick your foot on the lead as well to help them go down, this way they have nowhere to go except down. You will find this hard as any dog does not like submitting to anything. With this you need to be focused. If the dog starts getting stressed then relax and take a break then start again. Remember to give lots of praise when your dog does go down.

Another quick way is to as you're walking your dog suddenly without warning do as above quickly. As soon as they have gone down start walking again, take 5 or 6 steps, then do the same again. Do this in quick successions so you are not giving your dog time to think. They will eventually get the message and give in.

When your dog eventually goes down practise whilst walking along the street and just say down and see what happens. But remember praise when they go down.

Key Points
Hold lead in left hand by collar
Pull down gently
Say down in firm voice
Step on lead if need to
Praise
C.A.P

HEELWORK

Heelwork is really important for you and your dog as your dog needs structure and part of that structure is you.

To start with always walk with the dog on your left, reason for this is it's giving your dog something to do and is part of your structure. Hold the lead in your right hand and hold your hand at waist height (as in FIGURE 1).

FIGURE 1

Do not hold the lead with the left hand unless you have problems with your right hand. You only need the left hand for correction purposes.

There are a few methods which you can use to stop your dog pulling:

Method 1

Before you start to walk make sure your dog is by your left leg, then with your left leg take a big stride and tell your dog to HEEL before you step off (FIGURE 2).

 FIGURE 2

When your dog starts to pull STOP!! Then pull your dog back to your left leg and make him/her sit then carry on, repeat as necessary. This might take a few attempts, but its persistence and your dog will learn that he/she is not going to get very far if they keep pulling. When your dog is walking to heel, praise them for doing so.

Method 2

As before keep your dog on your left and lead in right hand and a big step before moving off and telling him/her to heel before you step off. As soon as your dog starts to pull grab hold of the lead with the left hand and pull back to your left leg. (FIGURE 1). C.A.P.

FIGURE 1

You don't need to pull back hard, just enough to give them a bit of a shock but depending what sort of dog you have depends on how hard you pull.

When you pull back on the lead tell them to heel, when they are by your left leg and as soon as you have corrected them let go with the left hand and relax and praise when walking by your left leg. Your dogs front legs should be level with yours when walking if they start to get in front again, repeat as necessary, look for a nice loose lead, do not keep the lead tight as this will make your dog pull even more.

Key Points
Dog on left
Lead in right hand
Say heel before stepping off
Big step with left leg
Grab with left hand when pulling
Pull back to left leg
Tell to heel
Let go with left hand
Praise
C.A.P

Method 3:

As all above hold lead in right hand walk dog on left, as soon as starts pulling grab the lead with the left hand and turn around 180 degrees and walk the other way for about five steps then turn around again and walk the other way as normal. Don't say nothing to your dog just do a complete 180 on yourself and repeat as necessary.

This will get your dog thinking what are you going to do next and as soon as they walk to heel praise them as usual. Let the dog follow you, don't let your dog dictate to you which way you want to go, you are the alpha male/female.

Key Points
Dog on left
Lead in right hand
Say heel before stepping off
Big step with left leg
Do a 180 degree turn when pulling
Take 5 steps
Turn again
Praise
C.A.P

SLOW & QUICK PACE

Slow and quick pace can help you when walking your dog to heel. Also if you're walking around a boot sale or fete or you need to cross a road in a hurry then your dog will need to learn different walking paces.

To do slow, all you need to do is simply hold the lead as before and slow down to a crawl and tell your dog to slow. Do not let your dog dictate the pace as you might find yourself getting faster so keep slow as if you are coming to a stop. If your dog gets in front pull him back so his shoulders are by your left leg. Dogs do not like walking slow so this may be uncomfortable for them but keep at it and praise when doing well.

Quick pace is the same except tell your dog quick and walk as quick as you can nearly in to a trot. You will find that your dog like walking faster as it is more comfortable for them, just look at their tail, this will probably be in the air. Remember to praise your dog when doing well.

Slow tail behind

Quick tail up

Key Points Slow Pace
Dog on left
Say slow then walk slow
Pull back if gets too far in front
Don't let your dog dictate the speed
Praise when done
C.A.P

Key Points Quick Pace
Dog on left
Say quick then move
Praise when done
C.A.P

THE STAND

The stand is a very useful thing for your dog to do. Sometimes when you are walking along rather than making the dog sit you might need them to stand. For example, if you are at a kerb and there is glass on the floor you wont want him sitting on that.

Also if it's been raining hard you don't want your dog to sit in a puddle as you wouldn't would you. So stand comes in very handy.

To start with while you are walking your dog say to him staaaaaaaaaaaaand extending the A in the stand. Then just rub your hand from the neck to their tale whilst saying staaaaaaaaaaaaand. This will take you about five minutes to master.

Key Points
Dog on left
Extend the A in staaaaaaaaaaaand
Rub your hand from neck to tail
Praise when doing stand
C.A.P

LEFT AND RIGHT TURNS

Left and right turns are part of giving your dog structure in the obedience side of things, also it helps you to control your dog, as turning or doing something unexpected makes your dog think of what you are doing next. So they will keep and eye on you and not what's going on around them.

The left turn is a straight forward ninety degree turn to your left saying the word "back". Don't be afraid to walk into your dog as he will move anyway. If they do not move then walk into them. They will soon realise to look up at you for a command.

Right turn is simply do a ninety degree turn to your right and say "heel". Heel we have used before as this means follow my left leg. That is why when you start off walking to heel you take a big stride with your left leg and move so they will learn to follow your leg.

Another method you can try is picture a figure 8 where you are walking and walk around it. When you get to the top part of the 8 you will use back as you are going left and when you get to the bottom part of the 8 you will say heel as you are going right.

Key Points
Dog on left
Say back and turn left
Or heel if turning right
Do a ninety degree turn
Walk into your dog if you have to
Praise when doing well
Try a figure 8
Use above words heel and back
Praise when done
C.A.P

THE STAY

The sit stay is probably going to get you stressed out depending on how stubborn your dog is, but the key to this is not to give in. Set yourself goals and stick to them, if you give up, your dog wont so do not give up.

The first thing you need to do is make some time as this will be hard and frustrating, so stay calm and don't lose your temper.

Have your dog sit by your left leg, now with your left hand put your palm in front of your dogs nose as shown in picture.

Then tell them to stay and with your right leg swivel round and turn and face your dog as shown in picture.

Keep your left hand out straight with your palm showing and reinforce stay. Do not look at him at all, stay there for around 10 secs then return and stand by your dog and praise him for not moving.

If your dog moves then the key is to put him back in the same place where you started and start again.

Set yourself goals and stick to them like start off at 5ft for 5 seconds, then 10ft for 10 seconds. Remember 9 seconds is not 10, so if they move before you get to 10 start again but keep calm at all times and gradually move back and getting your dog to stay there for longer.

The longer he stays there the better.

If you have no joy after 5 minutes go for a walk for a few minutes just to relax your dog and yourself but remember the exercise is not over until you complete your goal.

Also what you can do is when you get further away from your dog call your dog to you as this will help on the recall as well but remember praise.

Key Points
Dog in a sit on left
Show dog your palm
Say stay
Swivel round and face your dog
Arm out straight showing palm
Do not look at him
Set yourself goals
Stick to them
Return to dog
Recall if further away
Keep calm
Praise
C.A.P

Leave

The leave is a very important command for instance if you're walking along the street and your dog sees a sweet and picks it up, you don't know how long it's been there or what's been sniffing it. So rather than your dog end up in the vets teach him to leave.

Also, if your dog likes to chase other dogs or bark at them or jumps up at people or even chewing you can use this command.

So, for starters practise with your dog by putting some toys down on the floor and telling your dog to leave in a firm voice so you mean it.

Once you've got your dog to leave indoors it's time to start outside and this is where the fun begins.

Dog on left as usual but what you want to do is find something your dog likes like sticks, tyres, plastic bottles and put them on the ground as shown in picture.

Then with your dog on your left walk around the objects down one side and up the other with a gap of about 3ft between you and the objects.

As you approach the objects tell your dog to LEAVE in a firm voice and if they go to pull towards the object pull them back and tell to LEAVE.

As you walk around the objects get closer and closer to them until you get close enough to walk over them. As you walk over them tell your dog to LEAVE but if they put their heads down to pick one up lift their head up and tell to LEAVE. But remember when they do leave plenty of praise is required.

Another method is using a plastic bottle, this is good if your voice activation isn't very strong. Get a small water bottle and put some stones in it about an inch full and it will work like a rattle. Use this when your dog goes to pick up and shake the bottle in front of your dogs nose but careful not to hit them and tell them to LEAVE.

Do not try to use this all the time as your dog will get used to it, but do use when needed.

 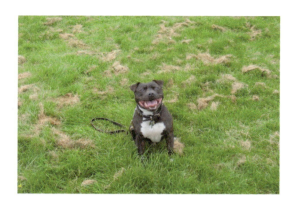

Key Points
Use toys in house
Tell to LEAVE in firm voice
Praise
Outside dog on left
Use some objects outside
Walk around objects about 3ft away
Tell them to LEAVE as approaching
Praise if leaves
Get closer to objects
Pull back on lead if need to
Lift head up if goes for objects
Praise when leaves
Use plastic bottle if need to
Fill about one inch of stones
Shake in front of nose
Tell to LEAVE
Praise when leaves
C.A.P

RECALL

The recall is not an easy task for some dogs as they would rather have a sniff than come to you. If you haven't got control of your dog on lead you are not going to have control off lead, so make sure you have complete control on lead before you set out of flead. Dogs associate with recall as going back on the lead and they don't like that, so you can try one of the following ways to get your dog back.

Firstly, get a lunge line about 20ft long and attach it to your dogs collar, this will give you control and safety if they do run off you can get them back.

With the lunge line let your dog have a run around just to get used to it then call them back to you saying your dogs name and COME. If they come back praise them a lot, if they don't come back reel them in like a fishing line so your pulling them closer to you and keep calling them using the word COME and be happy when calling them, do not get annoyed if they don't come back keep calm all the time. If your voice changes the dog will not come back as they will believe they are going to get told off give them lots of praise for coming back. Keep practising repetition is important as the more times you do it the easier it will get.

Key Points
Control on lead before of flead
20ft lunge line
Recall using name and COME
Reel in like a fishing line
Happy voice
Do not get annoyed
Praise
C.A.P

If you have got to the stage where your dog is comfortable on the lunge line and you are happy to let them off lead then do so but if your dog doesn't come back as he may sense freedom try these options.

The first thing to do is have your dog under control so try calling them back using name and COME also get down on one knee and pat your legs to get them back to you. If they come back praise them but do not put them on the lead at first and do not give them a treat.

Key Points
Call them using name and COME
Get down on a knee
Pat your legs
Praise when come back
Don't put on lead first time

If they don't come back then start walking away from the dog but don't call them. Eventually they will think why haven't they called me and will start looking for you and once they spot you walking away they will come after you and when they do praise them.

Also when walking dog off lead turn in a different direction to keep them guessing where you're going, as dogs get used to going the same route, so change it and do a left or right and let them come to you. Sometimes doing nothing and saying nothing is more effective than anything else.

Another thing is when off lead and you want them back stand still with your arms out stretched to the side and call them but as they get closer bring your arms in as shown in pics then get down on your knee and start praising them but it is a sign when you got your dog under control if you make them sit when they get to you so practise that.

Remember every time the come back praise them

Key Points
Start walking away from your dog
Turn in a different direction
Say nothing
Arms stretched out
Move arms closer when dog gets nearer
Make sit
Praise

BARKING

A dog barking is a sign of either stress or attention seeking or could be signs of aggression. As a responsible dog owner its up to you to decide which one it its.

If a dog is barking and running away it's a sign of stress and they do it to warn others off and could be a timid dog.

If your dog is barking and you tell it to shut up then it could be attention seeking, as they know if they bark you are going to give it some attention.

If it's barking at everyone and trying to get them and pulling like mad then it could be aggression and this needs to be sorted as they could be very dangerous.

If it's barking because it's scared or timid then what you need to do is get your dog socialised as the problem will be a lack of interaction with others. Go to dog classes for socialisation or to parks where there are people around but do it slowly bit by bit. Also do not tense up as the dog will pick up on that be calm and relaxed and praise your dog a lot so they feel safe. Remember you are their protector and they look to you for protection.

Key Points
Socialise your dog
Keep calm
Relax
Praise
C.A.P

If your dog is barking to get attention then STOP shouting at it when it barks. Ignore the dog every time it barks, don't even look at them and when they stop then you can give them attention. Do not lose your temper as you will have to start again but keep at it.

Aggression barking needs to be sorted first thing to do is go to your local vet and get them checked out to make sure they're ok. If all ok then to stop this you need to be a firm handler take control of your dog. If it's pulling to get to someone then tell your dog NO or LEAVE in a firm voice and use the plastic bottle if need to. Be assertive take control of the situation and relax, do not stress yourself out. When they stop barking then praise them. Also what you can do is if you are walking towards someone and they are barking then stop turn around walk the other way 5 or 6 steps then turn back again and repeat as necessary.

Key Points
Vet check
Tell NO or LEAVE
Use plastic bottle if need to
Be assertive
Take control
Relax
Stop turn other way
Repeat
Praise

JUMPING UP

Jumping up needs to be controlled as you don't want your dog jumping up at a child and accidentally scratching them.

If your dog jumps up at you when you walk in the house then it's because it wants to be greeted first before everyone else, and by greeting the dog first you are putting the dog further up the pack and before your family so that needs to stop. The two things you can do are firstly turn your back on them and cross your arms, if they keep jumping up keep turning your back on them and if you need to make a little squeak noise like a mouse then the dog will think it's hurt you so should stop. Everyone needs to do this when they come into your house and only when they are calm then give them praise.

The second thing you can do is walk towards the dog assertively and show you're in control and keep walking they will back down. Show you are in control be firm assertive you are the pack leader remember that.

If your dog is jumping up outside go back to the leave command and be firm.

Key Points
Cross your arms
Turn your back
Make a squeak noise
Walk towards your dog
Be assertive
Take control
Praise when stops

CHEWING

Chewing can be a sign of boredom as if you're out all day the dog is going to get bored or it could be attention seeking.

Do not tell your dog off if they start chewing something they shouldn't just tell them to LEAVE.

If they keep chewing then get some eucalyptus oil and dab it on areas where they are chewing as this stops them because dogs do not like the taste or smell of it.

Another way to help chewing is that people tend to give a dog too many toys at once, so see how many they have and pick them all up and just give your dog two toys a day and keep swapping them around.

Another way to help is get yourself a kong and put some cheap paste or some cat food if you have cats or some dog food if you feed them wet food, and put it in the freezer overnight and give it to your dog it will keep them busy for hours.

Key Points
Tell them to leave
Eucalyptus oil
Pick up toys
Two toys per day
Get a kong
Put in freezer

REMEMBER A WELL TRAINED DOG IS A HAPPY DOG

The End